Copyright © 2023 Krispy and Klean LLC

All rights reserved.

No part of this book may be reproduced, or stored in a retrieval system, or transmitted in any form or by any means, electronic, mechanical, photocopying, recording, or otherwise, without express written permission of the publisher.

ISBN-13: 9798399861760

Cover design by: Krispy and Klean
Printed in the United States of America

This book is dedicated to those who create without limit, remembering it is not the tool that creates but the one who holds it.

"A NEW BEGINNING A NEW TOOL."

Get ready to dive into the extraordinary world of AI-generated art! In this exciting journey, you'll be transported to realms where imagination knows no bounds and technology sparks new dimensions of creativity. Through a concise and engaging 10-step process, this book will guide you on an adventure that is both fun and simple, unlocking the full potential of AI artistry.

In the opening chapters, you'll discover the magic of specificity. By learning how to effectively communicate your artistic desires, you'll witness the AI breathe life into your visions. With just a few precise details, such as regal poses, enchanting surroundings, and mystical allure, the AI will transform your imagination into breathtaking masterpieces.

Simplicity reigns supreme in the realm of AI art prompts, and you'll soon learn the power of keeping it simple. Through the art of concise language, you'll unlock the ability to effortlessly guide the AI towards capturing the essence of warmth, tranquility, and captivating ambiance. The process becomes a delightful experience as you witness the AI infuse its creations with the emotions and impressions you desire.

Prepare to unleash your creativity by embracing the colorful palette of adjectives. By incorporating descriptive words that evoke specific moods, styles, and atmospheres, you'll guide the AI towards crafting art that resonates with your deepest sensibilities. Whether you seek haunting forests, whimsical gardens, or ethereal realms, the AI will transform your prompts into vibrant, immersive experiences.

As you continue on this adventure, you'll find yourself immersed in vivid scenes and captivating surroundings. Through the power of detailed descriptions, you'll be transported to bustling marketplaces, ancient moonlit forests, and enchanting realms bathed in ethereal light. The AI will weave these picturesque backdrops into its creations, evoking wonder and awe within you.

The journey doesn't end there. You'll be invited to explore the realm of color, where your preferences become the guiding force for the AI's artistic expressions. Whether you're captivated by the timeless allure of black and white or the vibrant symphony of electrifying hues, the AI will paint worlds that harmoniously align with your personal aesthetic.

Prepare to be amazed by the vast range of artistic styles and movements at your fingertips. From whimsical anime-inspired creations to abstract dreamscapes, you'll embark on a visual odyssey that transcends conventional boundaries. The AI will be your trusted companion, seamlessly blending aesthetics and capturing the very essence of artistic fusion.

Within each artwork lies a symphony of key elements, meticulously highlighted to create depth and significance. With your guidance, the AI will celebrate the intricate details, whether it's delicate porcelain vases bathed in ethereal sunlight or mesmerizing interplays of light and shadow. Every brushstroke will enchant viewers, immersing them in a world of sublime beauty.

Through the 10-step process outlined in this book, you'll witness the evolution of your AI-generated creations. From monumental murals that command attention to intimate miniatures that captivate the eye, the AI will craft artworks tailored to your desired size and dimensions. Your artistic vision will come to life, leaving a lasting impression on all who behold it.

So, get ready to embark on a thrilling journey of imagination and technology. With just 10 simple steps, you'll unlock the remarkable world of AI-generated art and discover the joy of witnessing your dreams materialize on the digital canvas. Let the adventure begin! g

" Chapter 1:This is a relationship: Be Specific In What You Want"

Being specific is the key! You need to clearly define the subject, theme, or concept you want the AI to generate. Ambiguity can lead to unexpected or irrelevant results, so be as precise as possible. Imagine requesting an AI-generated artwork of a majestic lion standing proudly on a mountaintop under a starry night sky. By providing specific details such as the animal, its pose, the setting, and the mood, you guide the AI to create a masterpiece tailored to your imagination.

Associated words: soar, blaze, vibrant, plumage, ascending, enchanted, forest, fiery, spirit, mystical, allure, surroundings, colors, patterns, majestic, pose, precise, details, masterpiece,

KRISPY AND KLEAN

ignite, imagination.

CHAPTER 1 PROMPT: PRODUCE AN ARTWORK SHOWCASING A BUSTLING CITYSCAPE AT NIGHT, ILLUMINATED BY VIBRANT NEON LIGHTS.

" Chapter 2: Don't make things hard: Keep it Simple"

In the world of AI art prompts, simplicity is your friend. Use concise language and avoid complex sentences when writing prompts. This makes it easier for the AI to understand your request and generate the desired artwork. Imagine asking the AI to create a charming illustration of a cozy café with a couple enjoying a cup of coffee. Keep the prompt straightforward and accessible, allowing the AI to focus on capturing the warmth and ambiance of the scene.

Associated words: solitary, lighthouse, stormy, sea, essence, resilience, unyielding, power, ocean, simple, concise, language, brush, focus, silhouette, crashing, waves, turbulent, skies, guiding light, clarity.

CHAPTER 2 PROMPT: CREATE A MINIMALISTIC ILLUSTRATION OF A CAT CURLED UP ASLEEP ON A WINDOWSILL.

" Chapter 3: If it's ugly, say so: Use Descriptive Adjectives"

Want your art to have a certain vibe? Incorporate adjectives that describe the mood, style, or atmosphere you want in the art. This helps the AI understand the overall vibe you're aiming for. Imagine requesting an AI-generated artwork that portrays a haunted forest filled with eerie shadows and mystical creatures. By using descriptive adjectives like haunting, mysterious, and ethereal, you guide the AI to infuse the artwork with the desired atmosphere.

Associated words: weathered, dilapidated, cottage, overgrown, untamed, garden, embrace, beauty, imperfections, descriptive, adjectives, worn, texture, unruly, foliage, rustic, charm, allure, hidden, uncover, hidden beauty.

CHAPTER 3 PROMPT: PRODUCE AN ILLUSTRATION OF A DILAPIDATED COTTAGE HIDDEN IN A SECRET GARDEN, OVERGROWN WITH UNRULY FOLIAGE.

" Chapter 4: Know the surroundings: Set the Scene"

If you want a particular setting or background for your AI-generated art, mention it in the prompt. This provides context and helps the AI create a more cohesive piece. Imagine requesting an AI-generated artwork of a bustling marketplace in a vibrant city. Specify details like colorful stalls, lively crowds, and a diverse range of products to set the scene. By painting a vivid picture of the surroundings, you enable the AI to transport viewers into a lively and engaging world.

Associated words: otherworldly, moonlit, forest, ancient, trees, tapestry, shadows, ethereal, light, paint, transports, viewers, enchanted, realm, set, scene, describing, moon's, gentle, glow, misty, atmosphere, whispering, breeze, mesmerizing, magic, architect, imagination, bounds.

CHAPTER 4 PROMPT: PRODUCE A PAINTING CAPTURING THE SERENITY OF A SECLUDED BEACH WITH CRYSTAL CLEAR WATERS AND PALM TREES.

" Chapter 5: Mention color preferences: Black and White, or Vivid"

"Got a favorite color palette? Let the AI know! The AI can

use the information to generate artwork that aligns with your desired color palette. Imagine requesting an AI-generated artwork with a dreamy, pastel color scheme evoking a sense of tranquility. Mention your color preferences, such as soft blues, gentle pinks, and creamy whites. By specifying your desired color palette, you guide the AI to create a visually cohesive and emotionally resonant artwork.

Associated words: bustling, cityscape, vivid, hues, neon, metropolis, pulsates, energy, urban, vibrancy, color preferences, contrasting, palette, black and white, electrifying, spectrum, lights, guide, brush, life, captivates, eye, sparks, imagination.

CHAPTER 5 PROMPT: CREATE AN ILLUSTRATION USING COOL BLUES AND GREENS TO PORTRAY A SERENE UNDERWATER SCENE WITH MARINE LIFE.

" Chapter 6: Anime to Abstract: Incorporate Art Styles"

If you're looking for artwork inspired by a particular art movement or style, mention it in the prompt. This will guide the AI in generating art that reflects your chosen style. Imagine requesting an AI-generated artwork with a touch of Impressionism, capturing the play of light on a serene landscape. By referencing the Impressionist style, you inspire the AI to produce brushstrokes that convey a sense of fleeting beauty and atmospheric ambiance.

Associated words: whimsical, vibrant, characters, anime, art, dance, abstract, dreamscape, seamlessly, blends, aesthetics, fusion, playful, styles, fluidity, brushwork, ignite, imagination, inviting, visual, symphony, transcends, conventional, boundaries.

CHAPTER 6 PROMPT: CREATE AN ILLUSTRATION WITH A STREET ART/GRAFFITI STYLE, INCORPORATING BOLD LETTERING AND URBAN IMAGERY.

" Chapter 7: Details matter: Highlight Key Elements"

If you want certain elements, objects, or characters in the artwork, mention them explicitly. This ensures the AI incorporates these crucial components into the final piece. Imagine requesting an AI-generated artwork featuring a whimsical carousel with intricately carved animals and adorned with colorful lights. By highlighting key elements like the carousel, animals, and lights, you guide the AI to emphasize these details, creating a captivating centerpiece for the artwork.

Associated words: still life, composition, table, adorned, exquisite, bouquet, flowers, delicate, porcelain, vases, ray of sunlight, ethereal, shadows, celebrate, beauty, intricate, details, highlight, petals, brushstrokes, interplay, light and shadow, urge, immerse, minutiae, meticulous, element.

CHAPTER 7 PROMPT: CREATE A DIGITAL ILLUSTRATION HIGHLIGHTING THE INTRICATE DETAILS OF A VINTAGE POCKET WATCH, CAPTURING ITS TIMELESS ELEGANCE.

" Chapter 8: How big should it be: Set Size and Dimensions"

How big should it be: Set Size and Dimensions"

Example: "Need your artwork in a specific size or aspect ratio? Include this information in the prompt! This helps the AI create art that fits your desired dimensions. Imagine requesting an AI-generated artwork that will be printed as a large mural for a gallery space. Specify the required dimensions, such as 10 feet tall and 20 feet wide, to ensure the AI generates an artwork that perfectly fills the intended space, capturing the viewers' attention.

Associated words: monumental, mural, stretching, vast, city wall, capturing, essence, community, inspiring, size, dimensions, specify, towering, masterpiece, intimate, miniature, guide, hand, scales, heights, imagination, resonates, surroundings, lasting impression, commands, attention, awe, perfectly tailored.

CHAPTER 8 PROMPT: PRODUCE AN ARTWORK DEPICTING A SERENE FOREST SCENE WITH DAPPLED SUNLIGHT FILTERING THROUGH THE DENSE CANOPY.

" Chapter 9: If you have a vision, share it: Provide Examples"

Imagine a futuristic cityscape where towering skyscrapers

blend seamlessly with organic architecture, creating a harmonious juxtaposition of technology and nature. Share visual examples or references that inspire your vision for the AI-generated artwork. Provide images or descriptions that convey the desired aesthetics, from sleek and modern designs to lush greenery intertwined with futuristic elements. By sharing your vision, you empower the AI artist to breathe life into a world that reflects your imagination.

Associated words: vision, visual examples, references, aesthetics, imagination, futuristic, cityscape, towering, skyscrapers, blend, seamlessly, organic, architecture, harmonious, juxtaposition, technology, nature, sleek, modern, designs, lush, greenery, intertwined, empower, breathe life, reflects.

CHAPTER 9 PROMPT: DESIGN AN ARTWORK THAT PORTRAYS A MYSTICAL PORTAL LEADING TO AN ALTERNATE DIMENSION OR MAGICAL REALM.

" Chapter 10: Be open and try new things: Experiment and Be Curious"

Imagine an artistic playground where rules are meant to

be broken and experimentation knows no bounds. Embrace the spirit of curiosity and adventure as you explore the realm of AI-generated art. Encourage yourself to step outside your comfort zone, to push the boundaries, and to embark on a journey of artistic discovery. Experiment with different prompts, iterate on the results, and revel in the serendipitous surprises that unfold. Unleash your creativity and let the AI artist be your accomplice in this thrilling exploration of art without limits.

Associated words: artistic, playground, rules, broken, experimentation, bounds, creativity, encouraging, explore, techniques, styles, unconventional, approaches, preconceived notions, evolve, iterative, processes, unexpected, open, magic, unfolds, dare, step outside, comfort zone.

CHAPTER 10 PROMPT: GENERATE AN ILLUSTRATION SHOWCASING THE RICH FOLKLORE AND MYTHOLOGIES OF DIFFERENT CULTURES, FEATURING LEGENDARY CREATURES AND HEROES.

ACKNOWLEDGEMENT

All photos prompted through this book were created using the AI Art Generator, MidJourney.
Remember that all promptexamples will reflect different results. So be patient and stay creative!

www.ingramcontent.com/pod-product-compliance
Lightning Source LLC
Chambersburg PA
CBHW040348220526
45473CB00009B/2812